# The
# Guide
# to
# WIN

Wael Badawy PhD

ISBN-13: 978-0-9938703-0-9
ISBN-13: 978-0-9938703-1-6 Electronic book

DEDICATION

To my wife Roya

and my children Saif, Seleem, Adam and Zain

without whom this book would have

been completed two years earlier.

To my Mother, Sister and late Father who believed in
me and inspired me to be who I am.

Wael Badawy PhD

# CONTENTS

Wael Badawy PhD

# ACKNOWLEDGMENTS

First and foremost, I would dedicate this book to my wife Roya.

I also thank my wonderful wife for the allowing me to spend much time in front of my computer.

I'd like to thank my parents for future gatherings as I'm sure they will all read it soon.

My business partners, especially to continue on in the Journey.

I thank each of them for the community they've created!

Thanks for everything. Thanks to the general community for using my concepts and providing great ideas and support via mailing lists; without this help I could not create newsletters and podcasts.

*You were born to win, but to be a winner,*
*you must plan to win, prepare to win, and expect to win.*

Zig Ziglar

Wael Badawy PhD

# 1. What is a WIN?

WIN is a three character word that consists of the letters "W", "I", and "N". In this chapter, we will define WIN. Before defining "WIN", it is always recommended to explore the different

$$W+I+N=WIN$$

definitions of WIN. WIN is a noun, verb, and adjective.

Win is defined as

- ***Win(adj)*** to gain by superiority in competition or contest; to obtain by victory over competitors or rivals; as, to win the prize in a gate; to win money; to win a battle, or to win a country

- **Win(adj)** to allure to kindness; to bring to compliance; to gain or obtain, as by solicitation or courtship

- **Win(adj)** to gain over to one's side or party; to obtain the favor, friendship, or support of; to render friendly or approving; as, to win an enemy; to win a jury

- **Win(adj)** to come to by toil or effort; to reach; to overtake

- **Win(adj)** to extract, as ore or coal

- **Win(verb)** to gain victory; to be successful; to triumph; to prevail

- **Win(noun)** *is* an individual victory. *For example*, Our first win of the season put us in high spirits.

- **Win(verb)** to conquer, defeat.

- **Win(verb)** to triumph or achieve victory (game, war, etc.).

- **Win(verb)** to obtain (someone) by wooing.

- **Win(verb)** to achieve victory. *For example*: Who would win in a fight between an octopus and a dolphin?

- **Win(verb)** to obtain something that is wanted. *For example*, The company hopes to win an order from the government worth over 5 million dollars.

- **Win(verb)** to cause a victory for someone.

- **Win(noun)** a victory (as in a race or other competition). *For example*, He was happy to get the win.

- **win, winnings, profits(verb)** something won (especially money)

- **win(verb)** be the winner in a contest or competition; be victorious "He won the Gold Medal in skating"; "Our home team won"; "Win the game."

- **win, acquire, gain(verb)** win something through one's efforts. *For example*, I acquired a passing knowledge of Chinese; I gained an understanding of international finance.

- **win, gain, advance, pull ahead, make headway, get ahead, gain ground(verb)** obtain advantages, such as points, etc. *For example*, The home team was gaining ground; After defeating the Knicks, the Blazers pulled ahead of the Lakers in the battle for the number-one playoff berth in the Western Conference.

---

According to the British National Corpus

**Spoken Corpus Frequency** Rank popularity for the word 'WIN' in Spoken Corpus Frequency: #1285

**Written Corpus Frequency** Rank popularity for the word 'WIN' in Written Corpus Frequency: #1086

**Noun Frequency** Rank popularity for the word 'WIN' in Noun Frequency: #1419

**Verb Frequency** Rank popularity for the word 'WIN' in Verb Frequency: #90

---

- **win, succeed, come through, bring home the bacon, deliver the goods(verb)** attain success or reach a desired goal. For example, The enterprise succeeded; We succeeded in getting tickets to the show; She struggled to overcome her handicap and won.

### Win-loss record

In baseball and softball, a pitcher's win-loss record indicates the number of wins and losses they have been credited with. For example, a 20-10 win-loss record would represent 20 wins and 10 losses. In each game, one pitcher on the winning team is awarded a win and one pitcher on the losing team is given a loss in their respective statistics. These pitchers are collectively known as the pitchers of record. The designation of win or loss for a pitcher is known as a decision, and only one pitcher for each team receives a decision. A starting pitcher who does not receive credit for a win or loss is said to have a no decision. In certain situations, another pitcher on the winning team who pitched in relief of the winning pitcher can be credited with a save, and holds can be awarded to relief pitchers on both sides, but these are never awarded to the same pitcher who is awarded the win. The official scorer of the game in accordance with the league's rules awards the decisions. The official scorer does not assign a winning or losing pitcher in some games, which are forfeited, such as those that are tied at the time of forfeiture.

**What is WIN?**

WIN is a three letter word that can mean any of the following:

- WIN is **W**ork **I**t **N**ow.
- WIN is **W**hat **I**s **N**ormal?
- WIN is **W**hen **I**n **N**eed
- WIN is **W**omen **I**n **N**eed
- WIN is **W**hip **I**nflation **N**ow
- WIN is **W**hat's **I**mportant **N**ow?
- WIN is **W**orkforce **I**nvestment **N**etwork
- WIN is **W**aste **I**nformation **N**eeds

## 2. Work It Now

The "work it now" attitudes about life is the secret of winning, and it refers to the ability to approach every challenge with a resolute commitment to excellence. It takes work to win, and you can't put it off until tomorrow. You have to do all that is necessary to win, and win today!

The state of mind of a winner is to know that "nothing in life worth fighting for comes easy." Sacrifice, effort, and sweat are synonymous with winning. If you look to see the attitude of a

> To WIN, you have to work hard in your personal development, and develop trusting and productive relationships with co-workers, friends, and family.

winner, observe how "easy" it seems! It only appears easy because of all the time and energy it took to develop skills and tools to win.

The winner attitude is:

1. Arrive early and stay until the job gets done.
2. Volunteer for the tough projects before anyone else.
3. Take pride in your work.
4. Enjoy the daily journey towards winning.
5. Expand your knowledge: take advantage of training seminars, ask questions, and read books.

The "work mindset," and the "now timeline" are the essence of the winner mindset; you never put off until tomorrow what should be done today!

Take action now!

Make it happen

Sweat now

There is no room for procrastination in a winner's attitude, and no excuses. In the stress and challenges of everyday life, it's so easy to become overwhelmed by countless responsibilities. Do not get strangled by seemingly endless pressures and challenges. Rather than take the necessary action to face these challenges head on, we may find ourselves immobilized and fearful.

It is "easy" to give in to the pressure and wait until

tomorrow to face today's challenges! However, many tomorrows can pass us by, and these issues may never get resolved. Do not remain uninspired and stagnant, failing to grow in your personal and professional lives.

The path to winning doesn't come easy. It is often strewn with defeat and frustration. Winning is often the function of relentless self-discipline, consistent training, passionate leadership, and a positive attitude.

It takes time, patience and dedication to win. You often have to stumble or take a step back in order to make a great leap forward.

> Hidden in every failure is a victory waiting to emerge. Never give up in your quest to be the best.
>
> Work It Now

### 3.  What Is Normal?

A normal personality, or normal behavior, is the key for becoming a winner. "Normal" literally means: 'according to the norm' or 'conforming to a standard." It represents an average, and by definition is dependent on a certain time and a certain culture. Normal is thus a function of culture, education, location, and other aspects, such as who you are dealing with.

Your personality should be independent rather based on subjective cultural or group specific norms when

Ethics is a special branch of philosophy, and is the study of the way we ought to live, what is good, and what is wrong.

presenting yourself. Your personality is related to your

ethics. It is about values and norms.

There is one universal ethical standard, valid for all people whatever the culture, society, or religion. Emotions, stress, and your cognitions (thoughts) are the interfaces between family members, partners, friends, or acquaintances.

All humans have common features such as a common heart or brain, AND all that we do and think is completely regulated by our brain. All things in nature work rather simply, and thus can be explained rather simply. Nothing is complicated! The thing is: we do not know everything yet.

A normal brain is responsible for a fundamental emotional memory system. We tend to remember

> All things in nature work rather simply, and can also be explained rather simply. Nothing is complicated! BUT we do not know everything yet.

(unconsciously) all kinds of things, such as our basic emotions—fear, sadness and anger.

Your personality consists largely of THREE fundamental building blocks:

1. Basic emotions: fear, sadness, anger and joy. Other so-called instincts such as lust also fall under these basic emotions.
2. Thoughts (cognitions), ideas, images, are expressed in our language and pictures.
3. Behaviour: all visible and observable behavior.

Instincts such as lust or sex, hunger, or aggression will be considered here as basic emotions. They all can be traced back to one of the basic emotions (sex to joy, hunger to joy, aggression obviously to anger).

These interconnect and form the basic emotions in your brain.

Your personality is built upon your sensory experiences and your basic emotions, and eventually on your thoughts. Based on an extremely complex network of thoughts (images or words), emotions and behaviors, our

> The feeling of what happens and to your "self" forms in your mind.

personality becomes a whole.

The emotional brain—where emotions and temperament are stored—and emotional outbursts are defined as being part of our "temperament."

But this is just an expression of our basic emotions, residing in our so-called limbic brain. This part of the brain includes a complex of several different brain parts: the amygdala, hypothalamus and pituitary (which regulate our autonomic or vegetative nervous system using hormones), gyrus cingularis, gyrus angularis hippocampus (memory), and the orbitofrontal cortex.

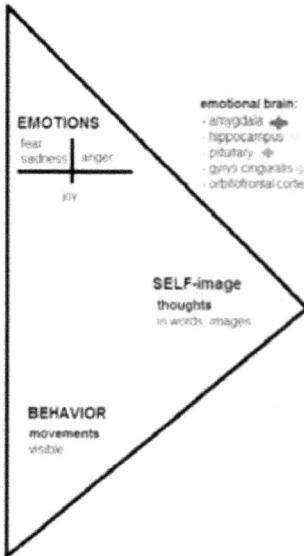

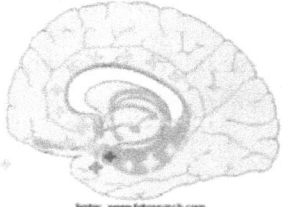

Personality

Brain areas

EMOTIONS
fear
sadness | anger
joy

emotional brain:
- amygdala
- hippocampus
- pituitary
- gyrus cingularis
- orbitofrontal cortex

link: www.fotosearch.com

SELF-image
thoughts
in words, images

neo-cortex:
especially frontal
and temporal lobes

BEHAVIOR
movements
visible

neo-cortex and
subcortical areas:
- premotor cortex
- basal ganglia
- cerebellum

Your normal personality is our so-called "self-image." It is made up of our thoughts or ideas about your self. As your self-image (also called the "self" or "ego") becomes larger, it becomes more complex and continuously expands.

The self consists of all our experiences, including our behavior and its consequences, our emotions, and our thoughts (also called concepts).

Aaron T. Beck believes that our self consists of 3 main layers:

- **Core-beliefs**: always starting with "I…" e.g. "I am smart"
- **Rules and Predictions**
- **Automatic thoughts**

The number of concepts (thoughts, images, experiences) continuously grows. As such our memory system keeps getting better and better to store everything. Logical reasoning and the thinking process also expands, so even more connections (either logical or illogical) are made from all our thoughts. This growth, however, increases the chances of making false associations or erroneous reasoning processes.

Every thought or concept or certain basic emotion is

always present and stored, at a specified intensity. Sometimes, even more basic emotions are coupled with just one thought. A basic emotion such as anger can be related (quite easily), but also sadness and even fear ... and in some also joy.

Your brain (your LTS) becomes a gigantic database of all sorts of images, thoughts, and emotions. It can be truly described as an extremely complex and large associative network.

The Big Five personality model

> **OCEAN**: Openness, Conscientiousness, Extraversion, Agreeableness, and Neuroticism are the five dimensions of a basic personality.

Our SELF-image has five basic personality dimensions. Every personality characteristic has a certain intensity, a certain strength with which it is part of someone's personality. The 5 dimensions can easily be remembered by the simple acronym: **OCEAN.**

**Openness**: Openness for new experiences, by some authors, is also described as Intelligence or Creativity. It refers to being curious versus cautious, or conservative versus innovative. In this dimension, you are open to new experiences, curious, adventure-seeking, and have high fantasy and high creativity.

**Conscientiousness**: It is SELF-control that represents the continuum of being efficient versus easy-going, organized versus careless/sloppy. This dimension refers to planned, self-disciplined, and dutiful behaviors. Being in control of your life, others, and your environment. Preferring clear rules and agreements, law and order. Here, you emphasize your conscience and a clear ethical system. Self-control is a fundamental human trait that is evolutionarily emphasized; losing one's self-control is usually very life-threatening in nature.

**Extraversion as opposite to Introversion**. It is the tendency to be outgoing versus reserved, energetic versus solitary. Extraverts clearly seek other people to relax with; they seek more energy or stimulation outside themselves. Introverts can generate their energy or stimulation from within, often preferring to be in a quieter environment. Introverts are much more sensitive to loud noises and many stimuli, they will feel overwhelmed much faster than extraverts. Their arousal-levels are already higher than that of extraverts; more external stimulation will lead much easier to an overload.

**Agreeableness or Friendliness versus Cold or Unkind**. This dimension refers to the tendency to being compassionate for anyone, and this is dependent on trust. If you do trust another human being, you will be unlikely to be more open friendly towards them.

> All personality factors can be traced back to the 5 dimensions of the Big Five model.

**Neuroticism** is a very unclear and non-descriptive word. It refers to emotional stability, the tendency to be secure or confident versus nervous or (too) sensitive. People differ largely in their capacity to remain calm under stressful conditions. Some become very emotional and almost hysteric, others seem to show no emotion and are fully in control. In neuropsychology, certain forms of frontal lobe damage do cause erratic, highly emotional

> You'll need failures to respect reality. Otherwise, you'll never learn to deal with failures and frustration.

behavior, whereas in others only flat emotions exist (actually not a form of emotional stability, but rather a serious disorder in which all emotions are absent).

### *Control and Worth*

Control is represented by conscientiousness, emotional stability, and openness. Worth is represented by agreeableness and extraversion. Wanting to be valued is more likely in extraverted people, especially in those who are more focused on what others have to say about them.

Self-image is built up of course by your successes in controlling your environment and in achieving the things you desire. The more success stories, the more the idea is strengthened that "you can do anything." And if others around you reinforce your successes, your idea of "I can do anything" grows bigger and bigger. Of course, the risk is that if this idea becomes too intense, then it moves further away from reality.

Self-image CANNOT be built up without any human or higher mammalian contact.

> You need a structure of rules, a norm and value system, and behavioral rules: ethics.

There are THREE core principles of personal human growth: truth, love, and power.  These 3 principles then are used to extract FOUR other principles: oneness, authority, courage and intelligence.

**Truth**: this represents our reality, as it is. Not as we would like to see it, but just as it is. Truth is seen as objectively as possible. To be able to see reality in this way, you need several cognitive and emotional capacities. For one, you need a correct perception, one not hindered by too intense emotions, a good planning and predicting capacity so you can predict reality effectively, a high degree of acceptance of your failures and successes, and a high degree of self-consciousness. Seeing the truth has a lot to do with having a highly developed self-image. For example, thinking too much that you can do anything, or that you know everything, will lead to failures in seeing and predicting your actual reality.

**Love**: In essence, this is the need to seek contact, making a connection with another living being. But it is more than contact alone; it is what all religions have in common: compassion. Compassion is the ability to empathically feel what another being feels or experiences. The deep connection you have with one person (e.g., your partner) is an example of an intense expression of love. Intimacy and sexuality all have a place in this. In this fundamental principle of love, the factors of agreeableness or friendliness of the Big Five personality model are represented.

**Power**: Largely misunderstood and equated with power to rule and manipulate people. In Pavlina's model, power is the strength within yourself to grow, to know yourself even better, and to change yourself and the world around you with confidence. However, this change is full of responsibility, focus, self-discipline, and the realization that true power has nothing to do with doing harm to others. Power is represented as being part of being in control or having self-control in the Big Five model.

The four principles that make up these 3 basic ones are also very interesting.

**Oneness**: this is the combination of Love and Truth. Pavlina believes, just as I do (and a lot of spiritual and religious cultures) that we cannot consider ourselves as different from other human people, or even other sentient beings. Of course we have differences, but the number of commonalities is much higher. And that when we consciously feel, we can feel the emotions of others as well.

**Authority**: perhaps a frightening word, but here Pavlina means true knowledge, of your self, of the world, and others around you. With power and truth, you'll become an authority on whatever field you are specialized in. This authority then makes you more powerful and thus more successful in reaching your goals. People around you will notice as well that you have the aura of wisdom, knowledge and inner peace, and strength. Without being arrogant.

**Courage**. A very nice principle I should think, as it's the combination of love and power. Courage is the ability to look beyond short-term goals or wishes to focus on longer term goals. Love is needed to connect and commit yourself to others, to their well-being. Without such a connection, no heroism is possible. Courage also has a lot to do with the absence of too much fear, and that has a lot to do with having sufficient power

When everything is ideal in the upbringing of a human being, in the physical growth of their brain, then they would grow in all 3 basic principles. They will need a healthy brain and the right kind of upbringing and education that teaches them from the beginning to acknowledge reality as it is.

All humans need the character feature of openness: being able to open yourself constantly for new things and experiences. Emotionally you'll need not too much fear; your fear has to be moderate enough not to be paralyzed by new things. In this way, you can step forward, encounter new things, and explore them. Being able to step into a dark forest and search for new adventures is just one example. You'll need enough curiosity as well, to overcome any fear you might have. In addition, your self-confidence should be sufficient in order to counter any threats you might face.

Improve yourself: start recognizing your personality disorders!

# 4. When In Need

What is the greatest need that you're facing today? Whether it is to feel accepted, to be forgiven, or if you have financial concerns, your heavenly Father is waiting for you to turn to Him.

If you're one of the many business owners spinning numerous plates and single-handedly tackling everything that needs doing, or indeed if you're a consultant helping said business owners in areas outside their expertise, how does this top 10 list resonate with you?

We live in rapidly changing times, especially for businesses. Consider that, in a single generation, businesses have had to adapt to entirely new marketing channels (the web and social media), decide how to invest in and utilize new technologies, and compete on a global stage—things that were barely imaginable to our parents' and grandparents' generations.

One side effect of these rapid changes and growth is that no single CEO—or any employee, for that matter—can be an expert in everything. This was, perhaps, always true, but it has never been more apparent.

This is why, in my opinion, some of the biggest challenges businesses face today are best met and addressed by using qualified consultants. Bringing on a consultant helps CEOs add the expertise and skills they need to address particular problems at particular times, and can provide the best possible outcomes.

Just a few of the challenges I see businesses facing that are best addressed with the help of a consultant include the following.

## Uncertainty about the future

Being able to predict customer trends, market trends, etc. is vital to a changing economic climate, but not every CEO has Warren Buffett-like predictive powers. Bringing in a consultant trained in reading and predicting these all-important trends could be the difference between a bright future and a murky one.

## Financial management

Many CEOs I know are ideas people; that means they're great at the big picture and disruptive thinking, but less good with things like cash flow, profit margins, reducing costs, financing, etc. Small and medium businesses may not require a full-time CFO, but would do better to employ a financial consultant who can step into the role as needed.

## Monitoring performance

Using a meaningful set of rounded performance indicators that provide the business with insights about how well it is performing is key. Most business people I know are not experts in how to develop key performance indicators (KPIs), how to avoid key pitfalls, and how to best communicate metrics so that they can inform the decision-making process. In most cases, companies rely on overly simple finance indicators that just clog up the corporate reporting channels.

## Business metrics matter

Business metrics are used to measure how successful a company is, and how well it is performing. This is why metrics are also important for management consultants. Any business consulting engagement should be measurable and, hopefully, impact some of the key business metrics of an organisation. The big question is, which ones are the most important?

We seem to live in a world saturated with data, metrics, and performance reports. Our corporate rivers are overflowing, drenching everything in numbers and targets, drowning us in data, while leaving us gasping for insights.

I have helped hundreds of companies, from major international blue chips to small family-owned business, develop KPIs. KPIs refer to "Key Performance Indicators," and most companies and government organisations are either drowning in them, and then using them so badly that they lead to unintended behaviours.

What I have learned over the years in working with companies is that there are four KPIs that are crucial for any business, or indeed any government organisation.

The four KPIs that come out of every workshop are the same KPIs that come out of every workshop I run with executives from all over the world, across all different types of industries. To get to them, I create a simple exercise and say to them:

"You are running this business and want to understand how well the business is performing. You now have to select KPIs for the business, and those metrics are the only management information you can use to judge whether the business is doing well or not. The challenge is that you have to agree on only four, and together they should give you a complete picture."

This, by the way, is a great exercise you can do in your company, with your team, or your clients and is one that sits in stark contrast to the way KPIs are usually developed: Brainstorming what we could measure and end up in a position where we measure everything that walks and moves—and nothing that matters!

Anyway, the four main KPIs that always come out of

these workshops are:

1. Financial Performance Index
2. Customer Satisfaction
3. Internal Process Quality
4. Employee Satisfaction

Here are the reasons why these KPIs are picked time and time again.

## Financial Performance Index

Money matters to any organisation. A publicly listed business needs to ensure it satisfies shareholders by delivering turnover growth and healthy profits, and not-for-profits or government bodies have to demonstrate that they provide value for money to the tax payer. Small businesses have to watch their cash flow, and even internal functions have to ensure they control costs and efficiently generate savings. The key metrics to use as a financial performance index are: sales growth, net profit margin, and cash flow.

## Customer Satisfaction

Without customers, companies wouldn't exist; all organisations have customers they have to satisfy. For example, large commercial companies have customers that buy their products or services, government organisations have customers they serve, and an internal function has customers (e.g., their co-workers in other departments) to whom they deliver services. Any business, government, or not-for-profit organisation has to ensure it delivers value to its customers. My favourite ways to measure customer satisfaction are: the Net Promoter Score, customer engagement, and customer retention.

**Internal Process Quality**

Companies need to make sure their services and products are to the expected standards and that they optimise the way these products or services are delivered. It doesn't matter whether you are a multi-billion dollar corporation, a not-for-profit body or a shared services function, all of them have to ensure their processes are as efficient and effective as possible and deliver the quality their customers expect. Here, I would recommend metrics such as capacity utilisation, project performance, order fulfilment, or product / service quality.

**Employee Satisfaction**

Even though I have written about the elimination of

human jobs through the use of artificial intelligence and big data robots, we can safely say that employees are the most important ingredients in any business. We all know that companies don't do well if their employees are not happy, and that this again applies to all enterprises. The people in any organisation are the ultimate drivers of success or failure. Ways you can measure employee satisfaction include staff advocacy scores, employee engagement, and absenteeism.

So here we have it. The four KPIs every consultant needs to understand. If you are seeking relevant and meaningful KPIs, simply start with these four and develop meaningful ways to measure and monitor them.

**Regulation and compliance**

As markets and technologies shift, so do rules and regulations. Depending on your industry, it can make much more sense to bring in a consultant to help with these areas, rather than trying to understand the complexities yourself—and risk fines or worse for non-compliance.

**Competencies and recruiting the right talent**

Again, a small or medium-sized business might not need full-time human resources or recruiting staff, but during peak growth periods, finding the right people and developing the right skills and competencies is the key to a sustainable future. Bringing in a consultant with the expertise to find exactly the workers you need is likely a wise investment.

## Technology

As technologies change practically at the speed of light, it's vital for companies to innovate or be left behind—but many CEOs started their careers and businesses before many of these technologies even existed! Consultants can be vital for integrating new technologies, especially mobile, app development, and cloud computing.

## Exploding data

Grandpa's generation certainly didn't have to deal with terabytes of data or worry about what to do with it. Indeed, 90% of the world's data was created in the past two years and therefore managing, keeping safe, and extracting insights from the ever-increasing amounts of data your company produces needs to be in the hands of a qualified professional who can help you get the most return from that data.

**Customer service**

In a world of instant gratification, customers expect instant customer service—and can take to the web to share their displeasure at a less than satisfactory service just as quickly. Consultants can find ways to improve customer service and bring it into the 21st century.

**Maintaining reputation**

In a similar vein, because customers can voice any displeasure so much more publicly and loudly than ever before, businesses have to monitor and maintain their online reputations. And while it's an important task, it's one best suited to a third party who can monitor and mediate with a certain amount of distance.

**Knowing when to embrace change**

Being either an early adopter or late to the game, consultants can help CEOs determine when to embrace change and when to stay the course. Not everything new is better, yet eschewing every change runs the risk of becoming obsolete. An outside professional opinion can make all the difference in these decisions.

We are living in an era of constant change for the

foreseeable future: change is the new normal. For this reason, preparing for and embracing that change by investing in the right kind of advice is the best way to meet modern challenges head on.

# 5. Women In Need

**Vision:** Our vision is that every woman has a clear path in which to achieve her desired potential and enrich her world.

**Mission:** To provide health and education grants to low-income women in Washington to help them improve their lives.

**Values:**

*Empowerment with accountability* — Taking initiative and accepting responsibility for the consequences of our actions.

*Respect with kindness* — Seeing the potential in each person and behaving in an encouraging manner toward everyone who touches the organization.

*Accessibility* — WIN is accessible to all without regard to race, religion, age, sexual orientation or physical or mental disability.

*Stewardship* —WIN commits to responsible planning and efficient management of resources so that we can sustain our ability to drive long-term impact in our community.

## 6.   Whip Inflation Now

In October 1974, with consumer inflation running at more than 10% annually, President Gerald Ford gave a now famous speech in which he proclaimed: "*There is only one point on which all advisers have agreed: We must whip inflation right now.*"

Dear President Ford:

I enlist as an Inflation Fighter and Energy Saver for the duration. I will do the very best I can for America

(Please Print)

Name_____ Date_____

Address_____

City_____ State_____ Zip Code_____

The White House released this form in Washington Tuesday which President Ford will ask American citizens to use to sign up as Inflation Fighters and Energy Savers and mail to the President's WIN Coordinating Office. A free WIN button will be sent to those signing up.

Watertown Daily Tithes, Wednesday, October 9, 1974

"Whip Inflation Now" was not just a speech—it was a public relations campaign to enlist American citizens to hold back increases in wages and prices in the 1970s, supposedly by increasing personal savings and taming spending habits. The symbol of the campaign was the large round red button with bold, white uppercase letters: W I N.

According to the American Presidents blog, "The campaign did not work as President Ford had hoped. Inflation remained a threat to the economy well into the Reagan presidency ... the pins were widely mocked, and it gave Ford's opponents an easy target for criticism."

In fact, by the late 1970s, inflation got a lot worse, as the "Inflation" section of PBS's "The First Measured Century" explains.

Macroblog posted a discussion about WIN in *Was WIN a Loser?*, in which Dave Altig debates whether the campaign was a failure. Part one of the blog post points to the need when discussing WIN, to distinguish between inflation and increases in the relative cost of living. Part two is a partial defense of Ford and his then-Chairman of the Federal Reserve, Arthur Burns, who were at the time challenged by "trying to learn how to conduct monetary policy in the aftermath of the collapse of the Bretton Woods global monetary system."

Nevertheless, the WIN buttons were a big deal, and the image invaded the popular culture. According to the blogger Rick Kaempfer, in a lunch meeting between President Ford and George Harrison (the Beatle, not George L. Harrison, the former President of the New York Fed!), the President gave the Beatle a WIN button, and George Harrison gave the President an OM (Hindu mantra word expressing creation) button.

The "WIN" idea carried over to Ford's run for President in 1975. At that time, there was a campaign button depicting the character Fonzie from "Happy Days," with Gerald Ford's face and wearing a "WIN" button with the slogan "Happy Days Are Here Again."

The image of the red button with the bold letters resurfaced in more modern discussions about inflation. In May 2003, Stephen Cecchetti (former Research Director of the New York Fed) wrote: "I'm thinking of going out and having a bunch of new red and white WIN buttons made and handing them out to the people attending next Tuesday's FOMC meeting." One blogger in 2005 wrote that "Stop Inflation Now" would have been a better slogan (just changing the first letter on the button).

You have to stop personal inflation; unnecessary spending and better manage your budget and expenses.

## 7. What's Important Now?

What's Important Now comes from the famous Notre Dame football coach Lou Holtz.

Holtz instructed his players to ask themselves this question 35 times a day. He wanted them to think about it when they awakened, while they were in class, study hall, the weight room, the practice field, standing on the sidelines during a game, and while on the playing field during a game. Holtz wanted his players to be able to learn to focus on what mattered most at any given time.

As an individual, we should ask ourselves this same question 35 times a day. In doing so, we would be forced to focus on what is important at a particular moment in time, enabling us to prioritize our mission, any threats, and our actions. If we have the correct mindset, we will then focus on what we need to do to win.

As a leader, we should ask ourselves this question because it helps us focus on what is important in our decisions, which areas of living or business need to be addressed and which have the highest priority. This focus is required for us to prepare us to be winners and warriors. Let us explore areas where we need to take a serious look at 'What's Important Now?'

You will always feel that you are pulled in some different directions at the same time. The three biggest competitors for your time include your financial life, family life, and spiritual life.

The challenge is where the three areas are allowed to compete with one another for our attention. While at work, you are worried about your family or your spiritual condition. While you are with your family, you are distracted by concerns about your job. While you practice your personal relationship in spiritual matters, you may wonder if your family or job is taking precedence over that important aspect of your life.

When you apply the principle, "What is Important Now?" when you are with your family, you give 100% undivided attention to your family. When you are at work, you give 100% undivided attention to your job, and when you are working on your spiritual life, you give 100% undivided attention to your spiritual life.

It is the most frustrating thing in the world to be in one place physically and another place mentally or emotionally. It will rip you apart. It reminds me of the quote, "Hard work has never hurt anyone ... but trying to decide which work to do has killed a lot of people!"

You see, you cannot be divided in your physical life and your emotional life.

Setup your priority and work out **W**hat is **I**mportant **N**ow?

- WIN  priority #1 _____
- WIN  priority #2 _____
- WIN  priority #3 _____
- WIN  priority #4 _____
- WIN  priority #5 _____

## 8.   Workforce Investment Network

**W**orkforce **I**nvestment **N**etwork represents what do you do to invest in your workforce. It is a function of what you do and what you would like to achieve. You should focus on your job employment, retention, earnings of participants, and increase your occupational skill.

As a result, you need to improve your quality and skills, reduce your dependency, and enhance your productivity and competitiveness.

You can ask the following simple questions to achieved this:

- Are you eligible to do the task?
- Do you select the right assignments?
- What are your activities?
- Do your activities serve you?
- What kind of support do you have?
- What is your operating plan?
- What are your standards of conduct?
- Do you participate in your community?
- Do you have access to an advisor?

Achieve and excel are your gateways to winning.

Questions you should ask yourself.

### Are You Eligible to do the task?

Define the task, goals, objectives and completion. Ask questions such as:

- What is the goal of this task?
- What are the first three objectives?
- When is the task complete?
- What is the risk to complete?
- What are the skills required for this task?

The biggest challenge is to identify the completion of a task. You should also answer questions such as:

- What does it mean to complete a task?
- How long will it take to complete a task?
- What is the outcome documents of the task?

### Do you select the right assignments?

Selection of the right assignments is critical to win. You must limit yourself only to tasks that you are prepared to complete.

**What are your activities?**

Your activities, what you do and how to do are key factors in your performance. If you have activities that are not related to your experience of knowledge you will be frustrated. Your frustration will kill your productivity. The main approach is to minimize your efforts and maximize your outcomes—this will enable you to win.

> Be a Red Apple and surround yourself with Red Apples, and don't worry about the Green Apples.

**Do your activities serve you?**

Your activities have to serve you and your winning strategy. Your activities have to serve your objective and your winning goal. A win will be achieved once you have passion, dedication, and are persistent.

**What kind of support do you have?**

You have to get support from your surroundings. This support can be in the form of moral support. The support has be complementary, and you need to be held accountable. Whenever you are aware that you are missing skills, you should look for a complementary skillset.

Like all aspects of life, and in business, we have different customers, each can be negative, positive, or neutral. We also have different employees who can be negative, positive, or neutral. We have different co-workers who can be negative, positive or neutral. No matter what is the example, we will always find red apples, green apples, and brown apples.

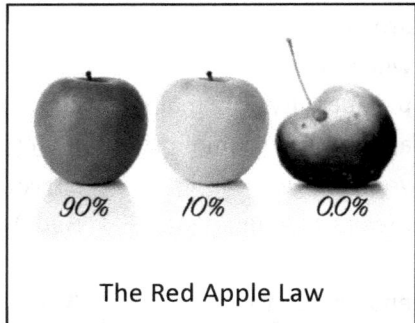

The Red Apple Law

The Red apples are the good ones, the delicious ones, the performers, the positive, the high energy, etc.

The Green apples are the sour ones, the ones who do not want to move, but they cannot decide, the undecided, I call them the "waiting for the train" for a ride or a hit, etc.

The Brown apples are the bad ones, the negative, the rejected, the non-performers, the road blockers, the negatives, etc. These are the bad influences, which can harm you.

To be successful, you must be a Red Apple, surrounded

by at least 90% Red Apples, with at most about 10% Green Apples. But avoid Brown Apples—have 0% Brown Apples in your life. Your goal is convert to Green Apples to Red Apples. If you are stuck with a Brown Apple, you will eventually be Brown.

*It is a Red, Red, Red, Apple; and only a Red Apple wins.*

## What is your operating plan?

Design an operating plan. Define your tasks and timeline. Define your check points and priorities. Everyone has a reason to hate operational planning. It takes too long. Worse, it takes all that time to do and is often forgotten. It gets confusing ("Isn't this more of a strategy than an objective?" Argghhh!). And even when everyone manages to drag themselves through all that, reporting on and reviewing the execution of those plans gets so boring you wish you were the ones being executed.

These problems come to mind now because I am advising a small, but fast-growing company doing its first round of real planning. The benefits are high. It is worth trying to reduce the costs.

The pieces:

- Strategy Summary

- Operating Plan Initiatives List

- Operating Action Plans

- Review Template

**The Strategy Summary**

This assumes that you have done the strategy development already. If so, you have a ton of documents with options, analyses, dreams, obfuscations, spider diagrams, and assumption-laden spreadsheets to show for it. Now you just need all of that exquisitely distilled into one page. "Impossible!", you say? We aren't exactly talking Shakespeare here; it can be done. And it really has to be done. Give every employee a single, digestible page that shows what needs to change and by how much and you dramatically increase your chances of accomplishing and exceeding that.

 The requirements for an effective one page strategy summary are:

1. *Whole Entity Goals:* There should not be more than 6 of these. These should indicate the actual numeric goal that the entity will achieve by the end of the planning period (a year, or

half year if you are in the midst of massive change). In this case I have suggested:

- A growth goal

- A profit goal

- A customer satisfaction or loyalty goal, and

- Some version of an employee satisfaction or engagement goal

2. *Strategic Intent Blocks:* No more than 5 strategy areas. In the example above I have 4 strategy blocks:
   - Markets and Products

   - Processes

   - Employees/Culture

   - Finance and Admin

   - Each one has:

A description of the key strategic intent. This is a pithy phrase that captures the key CHANGE that you will effect. If there is no change word ("increase" "eliminate", "accelerate", etc.), try again. (Remember, these are not meant to cover everything that the organization will do. They are the areas which require extra focus and will produce the biggest impact.)

The main tactical initiative areas. Keep these broad enough and phrased as objectives; let your teams figure out how to accomplish them. They will be more engaged, develop more, and are likely to do greater things that you would have thought of!

The very few key metrics—and associated specific goals–that indicate the size of the change needed and that will tell if you accomplished the strategy. Nota Bene: Always define the goals as a minimum (i.e., "at least" or "less than") rather than as a specific value. Research shows that people will just meet a specific goal, but will consistently outperform when the goal is open-ended. Go figure. Now you know how to increase your organizations output by 15% simply by learning how to type "<" and ">".

**Operating Plan Initiatives List**

Once the strategy is clear, your teams or functional groups can go off and develop action plans. Warning, warning! This is where the strategy can be undermined if people pursue all the projects they like, and fit strategic initiatives in edgewise. Negotiating to a 1-2 page list of all the major initiatives and their owners helps the management team drive the importance of focus and make clear trade-offs. You'll ultimately end up with a succinct initiative list for each function or group that contains:

*Initiatives directly in support of the strategies:* These are the highest priority.

*Initiatives for some ongoing obligations:* Some of these are essential, and some may need to be further examined or potentially dropped over time.

*Other initiatives:* If there are many additional initiatives, it is worth checking to see if they are justified, and if they can be done without jeopardizing the strategic items.

## Operating Action Plans

This is where functional or project teams lay out what they will actually do. There will be groaning, but you need to persevere. Writing it down gives you a prayer of a chance that everyone will be mobilized around a scope, a pace, and interim milestones such that they will actually achieve the desired outcomes. Without this plan, it is really easy to go forward with all good intentions, have 3 quarters of highly upbeat review meetings at which actions taken are reported proudly, and then in the 4th quarter notice that we are not actually going to produce the expected results. Explanations for the gap will abound. The fact is, if your teams can't describe at least one way to accomplish the objectives and let everyone see and critique that objective, your expected results have a high chance of being road-kill.

## One Page Review Template

That which gets measured gets done. So you need to monitor the execution. Quarterly is fine for the whole plan by the whole leadership team. (Other reviews of key projects should happen with the right set of people as they go along and reach milestones.)

• What are your standards of conduct?

A standard of conduct is a set of rules that outlines the social norms and rules and responsibilities of, or proper practices for, an individual, party, or organization. Related concepts include ethical, honor, moral codes and religious laws.

"Principles, values, standards, or rules of behavior that guide the decisions, procedures and systems of an organization in a way that (a) contributes to the welfare of its key stakeholders, and (b) respects the rights of all constituents affected by its operations."

A code of conduct is an important step in establishing an inclusive culture, but it is not a comprehensive solution on its own. An ethical culture is created by the organization's leaders who manifest their ethics in their attitudes and behavior. Studies of codes of conduct in the private sector show that their effective implementation must be part of a learning process that requires training, consistent enforcement, and continuous measurement/improvement. Simply requiring members to read the code is not enough to ensure that they understand it and will remember its contents.

•	Do you participate in your community?

Participation is a rich concept that varies within its application and definition. The way participation is defined also depends on the context in which it occurs. For some, it is a matter of principle; for others, practice; for others still, an end in itself.

Often the term participation is modified with adjectives, resulting in terms such as community participation, citizen participation, people's participation, public participation, and popular participation. The Oxford English Dictionary defines participation as "to have a share in" or "to take part in," thereby emphasizing the rights of individuals and the choices that they make in order to participate.

A descriptive definition of participation programs would imply the involvement of a significant number of persons in situations or actions that enhance their well-being; for example, their income, security, or self-esteem. The ideal conditions contributing towards meaningful participation can be discussed as follows:

1. What kind of participation is under consideration?
2. Who participates in it?
3. How does participation occur?

The following issues are important in order to assess the extent of community participation:

1. Who participates?
2. What do people participate in?
3. Why do people participate? There are:
   a) Cultural explanations (values, norms, roles, etc.)
   b) Cognitive explanations (verbal skills and knowledge about the organizations)
   c) Structural explanations (alternatives, resources available, and the nature of benefit sought)
4. Implications (how the benefit contributes to the ends or principles they value).

The last word, community participation, is defined as the process by which individuals, families, or communities assume responsibility for their own welfare and develop a capacity to contribute to their own and the community's development. In the context of development, community participation refers to an active process whereby beneficiaries influence the direction and execution of development projects, rather than merely receive a share of the project benefits. The five objectives to which community participation might include are:

1. *Sharing project costs:* participants are asked to contribute money or labor (and occasionally goods) during the project's implementation or operational stages.
2. *Increasing project efficiency:* beneficiary consultation during project planning or beneficiary involvement in the management of project implementation or operation.
3. *Increasing project effectiveness:* greater beneficiary involvement to help ensure that the project achieves its objectives and that benefits go to the intended groups.
4. *Building beneficiary capacity:* either through ensuring that participants are actively involved in project planning and implementation or through formal or informal training and consciousness-raising activities.
5. *Increasing empowerment:* defined as seeking to increase the control of the underprivileged sectors of society over the resources and decisions affecting their lives and their participation in the benefits produced by the society in which they live.


• Do you have access to an advisor?

No matter how ambitious or talented, we all have our blindspots—certain obstacles or hard realities that we fail to anticipate. Which is why we all need some sound advice from time to time. To get it, we must engage the right advisors along the way.

Perhaps because of their necessity, we're prone to throwing around the term "advisor" much too loosely. Many entrepreneurs assemble a Board of Advisors and then have no idea what to do with them. Similarly, industry veterans agree to advise businesses without any clear sense of responsibility.

An "advisorship" is much more than a mentorship; it is a relationship between a business and a third party that has a specific value to add. There is an implied sense of expectations and reward. Just as an advisor must invest his or her time to serve the business, the business must invest time into the relationship. But what comprises a really great advisorship? Let's take a look at how to engage, incentivize, and manage your advisors.

**How to Engage the Right Advisors**

Select advisors based on areas of expertise. Every business needs a dream team, but you can't hire for every expertise you'll need. Sure, you may need developers and designers, but how about experts in your industry, or people who have relationships with certain prospects that you can't afford to hire? As you identify areas of expertise that you lack, consider who might be able to help.

**State expectations up front.** It is best to have a contract that covers details regarding any form of equity grant or compensation, as well as whether or not expenses are reimbursed. Some entrepreneurs explicitly state the frequency of meetings, phone calls, and possibly the number of hours expected from a committed advisor.

**Keep a candid exchange**. Your relationship with your advisors should constantly be optimized through candid feedback exchange. Entrepreneurs should ask their advisors the question: "How can I better utilize you to help the business?" Likewise, great advisors always ask the question, "How can I be more helpful to you?"

**Have an exit strategy.** Most entrepreneurs I know say that their "advisors" have less than a 50% success rate. Granted, great advisorships are a two-way street. That being said, it is fair to expect that some of your advisors will flake out, change industries, retire, or simply be too busy to help. As such, it is best to define up front what happens if either party decides that it's not working out.

**Once you have engaged your advisors, you will want to ensure a productive relationship.** Advisors can become a burden—in both expense and time wasted—unless they are managed wisely. Obviously, a great advisorship is a shared responsibility between the leader of the team and the advisor. Teams must select advisors for the right reasons, engage them properly, and then manage and utilize them—purposefully and consistently—over time. In the spirit of advice, I reached out to a handful of legendary advisors and entrepreneurs that have experience on the topic, and asked them to chime in.

## How Can I Make the Most of My Advisors?

Guy Kawasaki, Entrepreneur, Former Apple Chief Evangelist, & Author of "Enchantment."

**Ask.** If you don't ask, you don't get. The reason you signed up advisors is because they are successful, connected, and knowledgeable people. This means they aren't idle. If you want their help, you've got to ask for it. You will sit by the side of a river for a long time before a roast duck will fly into your mouth.

**Know.** Basically, there are three kinds of advisors: "Mom" for adult supervision, "Jerry McGuire" for connections, and "Barack" for high-visibility window dressing plus those with specific technical expertise. The trick is to ask, or more accurately "use" each advisor in the right way. For example, using "Mom" to introduce you to Pete Cashmore at Mashable isn't going to work. Neither will asking "Barack" whether you should use RackSpace or Amazon Services. Figure out what advice you need and who can help you in these areas before you even recruit advisors.

**Pay.** If you're going to ask, you should be willing to pay. Actually, you should be happy to pay. An entrepreneur recently offered me 10,000 options in a company with approximately 20,000,000 authorized shares. A large turkey walking on the ground is more likely to show up on the radar than make an offer like that. 0.01% is where it gets interesting, 0.05% is where you're talking turkey. An advisor's magic number is $1 million upon liquidity. Assuming no dilution (which is not a good assumption), this means you need to sell for $200 million. If tenths of a percent of options for an advisor causes too much dilution, then you've failed anyway. You'll either make more than you ever dreamed or the company will fail.

Jeffrey Bussgang, General Partner at Flybridge Capital Partners, Author of "Mastering the VC Game"

**Hard, honest advice.** The best advisors give you the hard, honest advice—not just act as cheerleaders. Think Simon Colwell in American Idol, not Paula Abdul. Sometimes, you need be told you suck.

**Push AND pull.** Look for folks who are thinking about your company in the background at all times—sending you articles, making relevant introductions, asking probing questions whenever you send information out. It's great to have an advisor that "pulls" you into situations and dialog, not just folks who respond when you "push" for input.

**Respect.** Although many senior advisors may have more experience and perspective than the entrepreneur, if you don't feel like they're treating you with the proper respect and deference, don't waste your time. Some advisors get confused about their roles. They're not chairman of the board or a majority shareholder. It's your start-up. You can solicit input, but in the end, you make the final decisions and are accountable for the results.

**What Makes a Great Advisor?**

Fred Wilson, Managing Partner, Union Square Ventures

- When you advise a founder/CEO, understand that they will only take a small fraction of it.

- Advisory roles require face time. Regularly scheduled breakfasts are great.

- The advice given privately is taken more often than advice given publicly.

Gary Vaynerchuk, Founder of VaynerMedia & Author of Crush It

- **Under-promise and over-deliver**. Early on, when I was an advisor, I thought I could impact the businesses I advised in too many ways. Now, I try to under-promise and find specific ways to add value.

- **Keep the companies top of mind—always**. I use icons at the top of my computer for each of the key people/companies that I am advising. When I'm in meetings, I often take a glance and think about what I can do at that very moment.

- **Strike early**. Do something great for the company you're advising early on—whether it's making the connection for a new hire or key introduction, or helping them close a deal.

## 9.   What Is Next

The next steps are to be aware of the other WIN
concepts to your life. The following is a list that you can
consider.

- WIN   Welfare Information Network

- WIN   Windows

- WIN   Winter

- WIN   Microsoft Windows

- WIN   Water Insoluble Nitrogen

- WIN   Wine Is Not

- WIN   Women in Nuclear

- WIN   Wireless Information Network

- WIN   Work It Now

- WIN   What Is Normal?

- WIN   When In Need

- WIN   Women In Need

- WIN   Winn Dixie Stores, Inc.

- WIN   Warfighter Information Network

- WIN   Wireless Intelligent Network

- WIN   Whip Inflation Now

- WIN   What's Important Now?

- WIN   World Information Network

- WIN   Women's Information Network

- WIN   Western Integrated Networks

- WIN   Workforce Investment Network

- WIN   Wildlife Information Network

- WIN   Women's International Net

- WIN   Writing In Narrative

- WIN   What's Its Name?

- WIN   World Insurance Network

- WIN   Winton, Queensland, Australia

- WIN   Waste Information Needs

- WIN   Writing Improvement Network

- WIN   Women's Individual Nutrition

- WIN   Westlaw Is Natural

- WIN   Window file (FoxPro - dBASE)

- WIN   World Intercession Network

- WIN   Western Information Network

- WIN   Work In Newry

- WIN   Women In Net

- WIN   Way Into Nirvana

- WIN   Women In Numbers

- WIN   Western Integrated Network

- WIN   Women Involved Now

- WIN   Wireless Intelligence Network

- WIN   Waardensegmenten In Nederland

- WIN   White Indian Negro

- WIN   Work Incentive Credit

- WIN   Work Identification Number

- WIN   Women's Information Network

- WIN   Wisconsin Interstate Network

- WIN   Word In Narrative

- WIN   Women Inmate Nurturing

- WIN   What Interpreters Need

- WIN   West Islip Network

- WIN   Wyoming Independent Newsletter

- WIN   Women's International Net

- WIN   Winnebago Indian News

- WIN   Winning Individual Neighborhoods

- WIN   Walking Is Nifty

- WIN   WWMCCS Inter-computer Network

- WIN   Wales Ireland And Norway

- WIN   Words Images And Numbers

- WIN   Windows Icons Nuts

- WIN   Wake Information Network

- WIN   Workers Independent News

- WIN   Working Incident Number

- WIN   Woman's International Net

- WIN   Wildcats In Nature

- WIN   Western Industrial Nevada

- WIN   Whatever Is Necessary

- WIN   Wisconsin Involvement Network

- WIN   What I Need

- WIN   Wollongong Integrated Networks

- WIN   Write In Nellie

- WIN   Wash Identify Notify

- WIN   Western Intertie Network

- WIN   Worldwide Image Navigation

- WIN   Workforce Innovation Networks

- WIN   Wincanton (London Stock Exchange)

- WIN   Work Incentive Network (Companies & Firms)

- WIN   Working Image Network (Companies & Firms)

- WIN   Women In Networking

- WIN   Women Investing Now

- WIN   Wi-LAN Inc. (Private Company Symbol)

- WIN   Welfare Information Network

NOW, Define your own WIN and write it here. The most important decision you will make is to follow your own WIN.

- WIN _____

- WIN _____

- WIN _____

- WIN _____

- WIN _____

For more definitions and applications, please visit

http://www.TheGuideToWin.com/win

# 10. Win Quotes

"What does it mean to be the best It means you have to be better than the number two guy. But what gratification is there in that He's a loser—that's why he's number two."

Jarod Kintz

"You're not obligated to win. You're obligated to keep trying. To the best you can do every day."

Jarod Kintz

"One should always play fairly when one has the winning cards."

Oscar Wilde

"Winning isn't everything—but wanting to win is."
                                                Vince Lombardi

"For me, it's not about winning an award. It's also about not even being nominated."

                        Jarod Kintz, This Book Has No Title

"Never do a single thing in the anticipation to prove something to someone who has hurt you. If someone has hurt or offended you (whoever that person may be), never perform anything or strive for anything in your life with the mind of proving something to that someone/ to those people. May nothing that you do be done with any thought of them in mind. There is nothing that needs to be proven."

                                                C. JoyBell C.

"Dieting is the only game where you win when you lose!"

                                                Karl Lagerfeld

"There is nothing in this life that can destroy you but yourself. Bad things happen to everyone, but when they do, you can't just fall apart and die. You have to fight back. If you don't, you're the one who loses in the end. But if you do keep going and fight back, you win."

                                Alexandra Monir, Timeless

"Fame you'll be famous, as famous as can be, with everyone watching you win on TV, Except when they don't because sometimes they won't."

Dr. Seuss, Oh, The Places You'll Go!

"We're going to meet a lot of lonely people in the next week and the next month and the next year. And when they ask us what we're doing, you can say, We're remembering. That's where we'll win out in the long run. And someday we'll remember so much that we'll build the biggest goddamn steamshovel in history and dig the biggest grave of all time and shove war in it and cover it up."

Ray Bradbury, Fahrenheit 451

"I love teamwork. I love the idea of everyone rallying together to help me win."

Jarod Kintz, A Zebra is the Piano of the Animal Kingdom

"Often romantic relationships fail because you are trying to get someone to fall in love with the YOU that you never discovered."

Shannon L. Alder

"A quitter never wins-and-a winner never quits."

Napoleon Hill, Think and Grow Rich

"To be heroic is to be courageous enough to die for something; to be inspirational is to be crazy enough to live a little."

Criss Jami, Venus in Arms

"The real glory is being knocked to your knees and then coming back. That's real glory. Thats the essence of it."

Vince Lombardi

"This is not the end, this is not even the beginning of the end, this is just perhaps the end of the beginning."

Winston S. Churchill

"Not all dreamers are winners, but all winners are dreamers. Your dream is the key to your future. The Bible says that, "without a vision (dream), a people perish." You need a dream, if you're going to succeed in anything you do."

Mark Gorman

"Leaders live by choice, not by accident."

Mark Gorman

"Why would I want to win anything other than a beautiful game?"

Patrick Rothfuss, The Wise Man's Fear

"If you want to find the real competition, just look in the mirror. After a while you'll see your rivals scrambling for second place."

Criss Jami, Killosophy

"You rarely win, but sometimes you do."

Harper Lee

"Sometimes not getting what you want is a brilliant stroke of luck."

Lorii Myers, Make It Happen, A Healthy, Competitive Approach to Achieving Personal Success

"I have won."

Erin Hunter

"No matter how good you are, you're going to lose one-third of your games. No matter how bad you are you're going to win one-third of your games. It's the other third that makes the difference."

Tommy Lasorda

"Sometimes in life you don't always feel like a winner, but that doesn't mean you're not a winner."

Lady Gaga, Lady Gaga: Born This Way

"Winning has nothing to do with racing. Most days don't have races anyway. Winning is about struggle and effort and optimism, and never, ever, ever giving up."

Amby Burfoot, Runner's Guide to the Meaning of Life

"If you go looking for love you won't find it because love is never lost; only we are lost."

Shannon L. Alder

"I've wanted to win at everything, every day, since I was a kid. And time doesn't change a person, it just helps you get a handle on who you are. Even at age 41, I still hate losing—I'm just more gracious about it. I'm also aware that setbacks have an upside; they fuel new dreams."

Dara Torres, Age Is Just a Number: Achieve Your Dreams at Any Stage in Your Life

"Who you are tomorrow begins with what you do today."

Tim Fargo

"Humanity does not ask us to be happy. It merely asks us to be brilliant on its behalf. Survival first, and then happiness as we can manage it .... take what pleasure you can in the interstices of your work, but your work is first, learning first, winning is everything because without it there is nothing."

Orson Scott Card, Ender's Game

"Law is made by the winner to preserve victory over the loser."

Toba Beta, Betelgeuse Incident: Insiden Bait Al-Jauza

"Winning is a state of mind that embraces everything you do."

Bryce Courtenay, The Power of One

"If you lose your temper, you lose!"

Richard Diaz

"If you ask me how I want to be remembered, it is as a winner. You know what a winner is A winner is somebody who has given his best effort, who has tried the hardest they possibly can, who has utilized every ounce of energy and strength within them to accomplish something. It doesn't mean that they accomplished it or failed, it means that they've given it their best. That's a winner."

Walter Payton, Never Die Easy: The Autobiography of
Walter Payton

"It's easy to win. Anybody can win."

Philip K. Dick, A Scanner Darkly

"Opportunity doesn't make appointments, you have to
be ready when it arrives."

Tim Fargov

"Know you will win and you will win!"

Stephen Richards

"Obstacles are challenges for winners and excuses for
losers."

M.E. Kerr

"Some lean back. But those who lean forward are
poised to cross the finish-line first!"

T.F. Hodge, From Within I Rise: Spiritual Triumph Over
Death and Conscious Encounters with "The Divine
Presence"

"Winning may not be everything, but losing has little to
recommend it."

Dianne Feinstein, Nine and Counting: The Women of the Senate

"No one can take the shot for you."

Lorii Myers, Make It Happen, A Healthy, Competitive Approach to Achieving Personal Success

"Faithfulness imparts God's reason for all circumstances. No matter what the world says, losing is no longer an option."

Criss Jami, Venus in Arms

"Now I realized that me and him were just alike. We were both born to win. And, when we were not winning, it was OK 'cause we were busy planning to win."

Sister Souljah, The Coldest Winter Ever

"No man can be a failure if he thinks he's a success; if he thinks he is a winner, then he is."

Robert W. Service

"An insincere critic of a sincere person never wins."

Criss Jami, Killosophy

"You don't win a game by hitting the ball out of the court."

Carlos Ruiz Zafón, The Angel's Game

"How many seconds does it take to win second. As many as it takes to win first—if you don't use them properly."

Jarod Kintz, A Zebra is the Piano of the Animal Kingdom

"Games are lost and won in your mind as much as they are on the field."

Carl Deuker, Gym Candy

"Play to win because almost doesn't cut it."

Ana Monnar

"I GOT TIGAR BLOOD!"

Charlie Sheen

"Life is a game, you can't afford to lose."

Tracy Bleers

"I haven't celebrated coming in No. 2 too many times."

Mark Messier

"Win without boasting. Lose without excuse."

Albert Payson Terhune

"Where's the pleasure in bein' the winner if the loser ain't alive to know they've lost?"

Terry Pratchett, Witches Abroad

"Every man has a specific skill, whether it is discovered or not, that more readily and naturally comes to him than it would to another, and his own should be sought and polished. He excels best in his niche—originality loses its authenticity in one's efforts to obtain originality."

Criss Jami, Salomé: In Every Inch In Every Mile

"It is deeply satisfying to win a prize in front of a lot of people."

E.B. White, Charlotte's Web

"If I reveal myself without worrying about how others will respond, then some will care, though others may not. But who can love me, if no one knows me I must risk it, or live alone."

Sheldon B. Kopp

"Perfection of effort is not required, by the way. It is the consistency of attempting to work these tools that brings the progress. It's like anything else. If I want to tone muscle, lifting a ten-pound weight a few times every day will move me toward my goal much quicker than hoisting a fifty-pound barbell once a week. Yes, it really is true: "Slow and steady wins the race." Just try a little, every day. You'll see."

Holly Mosier

"There are no winners in real games."

Dejan Stojanovic, The Sun Watches the Sun

"Conquering any difficulty always gives one a secret joy, for it means pushing back a boundary line and adding to one's liberty."

Henri-Frédéric Amiel

 "If you do something that has never been done you will collect treasures that have never been found."

Jenna Newton

"Faith has won it! Fear has lost it! When you get full of

faith, the devil gets filled with fear! Keep your faith in light every day and you will keep the devil in fright always!"

Israelmore Ayivor, The Great Hand Book of Quotes

"The game itself is bigger than the winning."

Dejan Stojanovic, The Sun Watches the Sun

"I'd seen glimpses of a different me. It was a different me because in those increments of time I thought I actually became a winner.

The truth, however, is painful.

"In this life, you have winners and losers. the more you win, the higher you go."

Daniel Nayeri, Another Faust

"I train for the winning moments, hoping all those seconds off the clock will lead to firsts. I train for seconds, that's all—not even a cumulative minute—and that's why I only ever earn seconds. Still, I'd rather have time and silver than gold and sweat."

Jarod Kintz, This Book is Not FOR SALE

"When one person succeeds, we win as a group of

people. Support others dreams so we can all win."

Bianca Frazier

"The man who pulled my winning raffle ticket out of the hat said I was one lucky guy. I guess he didn't see me standing next to my clone, so I replied, "I am two lucky guys."

Jarod Kintz, This Book is Not FOR SALE

"If a woman named Ms. Silver won a gold medal, she'd probably be a little disappointed she didn't place second. My love always finishes first, while my love always comes second."

Jarod Kintz, This Book is Not FOR SALE

"Victories are won while on your knees! Keep praying for those who rise up against you. Fear not. The Lord has rectified the problem. Prayer is POWERFUL!!"

Anita R. Sneed-Carter

"Getting struck by lightning is like winning the lottery, only it'll ruin your life faster."

Jarod Kintz, A Zebra is the Piano of the Animal Kingdom

"An award would be more prestigious if it came with a

supplemental income for a year, so you could focus on repeating your title."

Jarod Kintz, 99 Cents For Some Nonsense

"I'm winning over fans every day. They're not my fans, but at least they're losing and I'm winning."

Jarod Kintz, This Book is Not FOR SALE

"Wars are won in the will."

Robert Fanney

"When you say you can't, you stop the creative powers in you; when you say you can you free them"

Bangambiki Habyarimana, The Great Pearl of Wisdom

"It is only normal that people count losses with their minds, and ignore to count blessings with the graciousness of their hearts."

Suzy Kassem, Rise Up and Salute the Sun: The Writings of Suzy Kassem

"You don't have to finish today, what is important is that you finish. But remember today might be the last day of your life."

Bangambiki Habyarimana, The Great Pearl of Wisdom

"Success is not a destination but a lifestyle."

Bangambiki Habyarimana, The Great Pearl of Wisdom

"It all begins with wishful thinking."

Bangambiki Habyarimana, The Great Pearl of Wisdom

"All you need to win is a winning attitude."

Bangambiki Habyarimana, The Great Pearl of Wisdom

"Don't fear defeat, expect victory."

Bangambiki Habyarimana, The Great Pearl of Wisdom

"Anyone can fall; but the winner always rises up."

Bangambiki Habyarimana, The Great Pearl of Wisdom

"Think you're a slave and you'll find a master; think you're a master and slaves will find you."

Bangambiki Habyarimana, The Great Pearl of Wisdom

"You were born a winner, a warrior, one who defied the odds by surviving the most gruesome battle of them all - the race to the egg. And now that you are a giant, why do you even doubt victory against smaller numbers and wider margins. The only walls that exist are those you have placed in your mind. And whatever obstacles you conceive, exist only because you have forgotten what you have already achieved."

Suzy Kassem, Rise Up and Salute the Sun: The Writings of Suzy Kassem

"Success is secondary to impact. Success is a list of what you win, gain and attain—it may pass it may remain. Impact is the test; the hearts, minds and lives you touch, enhance, and forever change."

Rasheed Ogunlaru

"Winner is Not Winner Until Someone Lose."

Yaganesh Derasari

"Nothing frustrates people more than a cocky guy who's still winning."

Criss Jami

"It was rather difficult to throw a game when you had no idea what you were doing to win it in the first place."

Brandon Sanderson, Warbreaker


"Focus all your life energy to whatever goal you set yourself to achieve."

Bangambiki Habyarimana, The Great Pearl of Wisdom


"Winning" is taking the talent or potential you were born with, and have since developed, and using it fully toward a goal or purpose that makes you happy."

Denis Waitley


"Plan strategically and strike it once to win. You can achieve maximum dues with minimum dice if only you are willing to clearly calculate and throw your efforts with optimism!"

Israelmore Ayivor, Daily Drive 365


"What is difficult in training will become easy in a battle."

Suvorov Alexander

"Don't expect others to hand success to you. Create it—with heart, energy and enterprise—and you'll make it come true."

Rasheed Ogunlaru

"Don't fear mistakes, they are your stepping stone to success."

Bangambiki Habyarimana, The Great Pearl of Wisdom

"Consider yourself a genius; you will be amazed at what you can achieve"

Bangambiki Habyarimana, The Great Pearl of Wisdom

"It's two things; you either choose to take risks through storms and win after the hail or you remain idle and die idle. Once laziness is deliberate; failure is not an accident!"

Israelmore Ayivor, Daily Drive 365

"No one can make you 'better' emotionally, mentally, spiritually or physically. You have to find this for yourself. You have to taste that brutal moment when you're crying in a corner of the room, curled up on the floor and you think this is your end. You have to fight to stand up, literally. And you have to walk over to your reflection and scream, scream it all out. Then you have pick up your sword and fight and never quit. This is your life. Don't let those bastards win."

Crystal Woods, Write like no one is reading

"When people want to win they will go to desperate extremes. However, anyone that has already won in life has come to the conclusion that there is no game. There is nothing but learning in this life and it is the only thing we take with us to the grave—knowledge. If you only understood that concept then your heart wouldn't break so bad. Jealousy or revenge wouldn't be your ambition. Stepping on others to raise yourself up wouldn't be a goal. Competition would be left on the playing field, and your freedom from what other people think about you would light the pathway out of hell."

Shannon L. Alder

"If swimming in gold were a sport, I'd be the Michael Phelps, and my winning would lead to more winning, as my gold made more gold."

Jarod Kintz, Xazaqazax

"It is not a person or situation that affects your life; it is the meaning you give to that person or situation, which influences your emotions and actions. Your choice is to change the meaning you gave it or to change your response, in order to create the outcome you want."

Shannon L. Alder

For more quotes:

http://www.theGuideToWin.com/quotes

# 11. ABOUT THE AUTHOR

Dr. Badawy is currently at the helm of IntellliView in the role of President and is navigating the company through commercialization into both local and international markets. He is also a world-leading researcher in video surveillance technology and continues to lecture throughout the world on his innovations. As a leading researcher he also oversees the evolution of the video surveillance technology developed at the University of Calgary and its commercialization in Calgary in order to serve and support Calgary businesses.

Dr. Badawy previously conducted his research at the U of Calgary, Canada where he was an iCore Chair Associate. Dr. Badawy developed a new model to describe optical video, thermal, infra-red, and 3D data in general. There he developed a model, algorithm, architecture and several platform implementations. These models have been granted several awards and patents, in addition to being published in numerous conference and journal papers. Dr. Badawy also trained and mentored researchers and engineers on his new technology, leading them to a successful commercialization path through a University Spin-off which housed 12 co-founders who worked in his research team at the U of C. Dr. Badawy's innovation and leadership contributed to Canada with:

• More than 400 technical papers that have been accepted for publication by the internal peer community, and a large number of citations that use this work, which currently exceeds 3000 citations.

• The 50+ contributions to developing the ISO standards, which represent more than 75% of the hardware reference model for the H.264 compression standard. Dr. Badawy led the development of the hardware reference model for MPEG-4, Part 9 in collaboration with Xilinx and EPFL. Also, he worked to develop several motion tracking architectures for low power applications that can be integrated into system-on-a-chip applications. This contribution impacted all international companies developing video products, as they have to use the developed reference model for standards conformance tests.

• Dr. Badawy was also listed as a "Primary contributor" in the VSI Alliance™ for developing the "Platform-Based Design Definitions and Taxonomy, (PBD 11.0), 2003". VSI Alliance is an industrial organization aimed at the development of a standard for IP Cores. This standard is used as a reference by all companies developing electronic chips for different applications, though mainly for communications and video.

• The impact of his publications has an h-index of 10 according to SCOPUS.COM, with the largest number of citations being 59, with total citations being 278, and about 1000 citations in Google. His success is product of his willingness to accept responsibility.

• The commercialization of a Canadian Video technology through a spin-off company IntelliView Technologies Inc.

All of this training, knowledge and technology that Dr. Badawy has transferred over the last ten years is seen in his students (about 2,000 undergraduate and 50 graduate), who are now contributing to the engineering field in different capacities, ranging from design, teaching, supervising, and manufacturing in several electronic components.